THIS IS WHY YOU'RE MINE

**A BOOK OF ALL THE THINGS I ADMIRE
ABOUT YOU... AND US**

TANGOBIRDPUBLISHING

"WHOEVER GIVES NOTHING,
HAS NOTHING.
THE GREATEST MISFORTUNE
IS NOT TO BE UNLOVED,
but not to love."

-*Albert Camus*

THIS LOVE STORY
belongs to...

MY VERY FIRST IMPRESSION OF YOU WAS...

♥

MY VERY FIRST IMPRESSION OF
YOU WAS...

ONE OF MY FAVORITE EARLY MEMORIES WE HAD...

♥

ONE OF MY FAVORITE EARLY MEMORIES
WE HAD...

"THE MYSTERY OF HUMAN EXISTENCE LIES NOT IN JUST STAYING ALIVE, BUT IN FINDING SOMETHING TO LIVE FOR."

-Fyodor Dostoevsky

A MOMENT I KNEW YOU WERE DIFFERENT THAN EVERYONE ELSE...

♥

A MOMENT I KNEW YOU WERE DIFFERENT THAN EVERYONE ELSE...

I REALIZED YOU WERE GOING TO REALLY MATTER IN MY LIFE WHEN...

♥

I REALIZED YOU WERE GOING TO REALLY MATTER IN MY LIFE WHEN...

A TIME YOU SHOWED UP FOR ME IN A WAY I DIDN'T EXPECT WAS...

♥

A TIME YOU SHOWED UP FOR ME IN A WAY I DIDN'T EXPECT WAS...

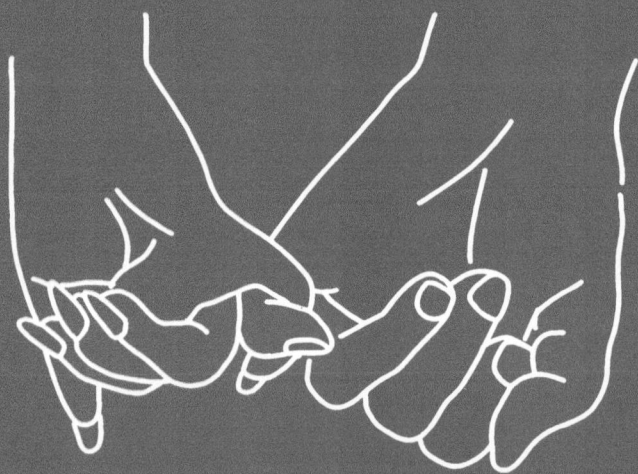

"LOVE IS THE ONLY SANE AND SATISFACTORY ANSWER TO THE PROBLEM OF HUMAN EXISTENCE."

- Erich Fromm

MY FAVORITE DATE WE'VE EVER HAD WAS...

♥

MY FAVORITE DATE WE'VE
EVER HAD WAS...

A DATE IDEA
I STILL WANT US
TO TRY IS...

♥

A DATE IDEA I STILL WANT
US TO TRY IS...

"WE ACCEPT THE LOVE WE THINK WE DESERVE."

- Stephen Chbosky

THE MOST SPECIAL PLACE WE'VE BEEN TOGETHER IS...

♥

THE MOST SPECIAL PLACE
WE'VE BEEN TOGETHER IS...

A PLACE I'VE ALWAYS WANTED TO GO WITH YOU IS...

♥

A PLACE I'VE ALWAYS
WANTED TO GO WITH YOU IS...

YOU'VE GENUINELY CHANGED MY LIFE FOR THE BETTER BECAUSE...

♥

YOU'VE GENUINELY CHANGED
MY LIFE FOR THE BETTER BECAUSE...

"TO LOVE ANOTHER PERSON IS TO SEE THE FACE OF GOD."

- Victor Hugo

BECAUSE OF YOU, I NOW BELIEVE...

♥

BECAUSE OF YOU,
I NOW BELIEVE...

A GOAL
I WOULD LOVE US
TO ACHIEVE
TOGETHER IS...

♥

A GOAL I WOULD LOVE US TO ACHIEVE TOGETHER IS...

AN OUTLOOK ON LIFE YOU HAVE THAT I LOVE IS...

♥

AN OUTLOOK ON LIFE YOU HAVE THAT I LOVE IS...

A MOMENT
I WISHED
I COULD STAY IN
FOREVER WITH
YOU WAS...

♥

A MOMENT I WISHED I COULD STAY IN FOREVER WITH YOU WAS...

"LOVE IS A CANVAS FURNISHED BY NATURE AND EMBROIDERED BY IMAGINATION."

- Voltaire

NOTHING COMPARES TO WATCHING YOU...

♥

NOTHING COMPARES TO
WATCHING YOU...

A PROMISE I WANT TO MAKE TO YOU IS...

♥

A PROMISE I WANT TO MAKE
TO YOU IS...

A RANDOM DETAIL ABOUT YOU THAT I LOVE IS...

♥

A RANDOM DETAIL ABOUT YOU
THAT I LOVE IS...

I COULD LISTEN TO YOU TALK FOREVER ABOUT...

♥

I COULD LISTEN TO YOU TALK FOREVER ABOUT...

"THE GIVING OF LOVE IS AN EDUCATION IN ITSELF."

- Eleanor Roosevelt

A MEMORY OF US I'LL NEVER GET TIRED OF TELLING IS...

♥

A MEMORY OF US I'LL NEVER GET TIRED OF TELLING IS...

THE SMALLEST THING YOU DO THAT I SECRETLY ADORE IS...

♥

THE SMALLEST THING YOU DO THAT
I SECRETLY ADORE IS...

IF I COULD RELIVE ONE NIGHT WITH YOU, IT WOULD BE...

♥

IF I COULD RELIVE ONE NIGHT WITH YOU, IT WOULD BE...

"THE DEMAND FOR LOVE IS THE GREATEST HUNGER OF THE HUMAN SPIRIT."

- Augustine of Hippo

SOMETHING YOU'VE DONE THAT MADE ME PROUD OF YOU IS...

♥

SOMETHING YOU'VE DONE THAT MADE ME PROUD OF YOU IS...

WHEN I THINK OF US 10 YEARS DOWN THE LINE I IMAGINE US...

♥

WHEN I THINK OF US 10 YEARS DOWN THE LINE I IMAGINE US...

A TIME WE LAUGHED THE HARDEST WAS...

♥

A TIME WE LAUGHED THE HARDEST WAS...

MY FAVORITE MEAL WE'VE EVER SHARED WAS...

♥

MY FAVORITE MEAL WE'VE EVER SHARED WAS...

"LOVE IS OUR TRUE DESTINY. WE DO NOT FIND THE MEANING OF LIFE BY OURSELVES ALONE — WE FIND IT WITH ANOTHER."

- Thomas Merton

MY FAVORITE THING ABOUT YOU PHYSICALLY IS...

♥

MY FAVORITE THING ABOUT YOU PHYSICALLY IS...

A PART OF YOU
I HOPE NEVER
CHANGES IS...

♥

A PART OF YOU I HOPE NEVER CHANGES IS...

MY FAVORITE INSIDE JOKE WE HAVE IS...

♥

MY FAVORITE INSIDE JOKE
WE HAVE IS...

SOMETHING YOU'VE TAUGHT ME ABOUT LOVE IS...

♥

SOMETHING YOU'VE TAUGHT ME
ABOUT LOVE IS...

_____

_____

_____

_____

_____

_____

_____

_____

_____

_____

_____

_____

_____

_____

_____

_____

"LOVE IS THE DIFFICULT AWARENESS THAT ANOTHER'S REALITY IS AS REAL AS ONE'S OWN."

- Iris Murdoch

SCAN BELOW FOR EXCLUSIVE ACCESS, CONTENT, BONUSES, SURPRISES & MORE...

@TANGOBIRDPUBLISHING